At Home with the Sacraments
Confirmation

PEG BOWMAN

At Home with the
SACRAMENTS
Confirmation

TWENTY-THIRD PUBLICATIONS
Mystic, Connecticut

Third printing 1995

Twenty-Third Publications
P.O. Box 180
185 Willow Street
Mystic, CT 06355
(203) 536-2611
800-321-0411

ISBN 0-89622-477-5

Contents

To Maureen McLain,
co-catechist and friend
and
to the students in my 1991 confirmation class:
Andrew, Brian, Dan, Michele,
Ryan, Scott, Terry, and Vickie
with gratitude for all that they have taught me

Introduction

It is always nice to feel "at home." When something out of the ordinary happens, however, we are sometimes thrown off guard, into unfamiliar territory.

This can easily happen when we participate in programs and celebrations at church. We usually feel at home at Sunday Mass, but when it comes to helping our children prepare to receive one of the sacraments, we often end up feeling uncomfortable and unsure of ourselves.

Most parishes have programs for parents before their children receive baptism, eucharist, reconciliation, or confirmation. Often these programs are mandatory—a child will not be permitted to receive the sacrament unless at least one parent attends. Sometimes these programs take several sessions to complete. Why are such programs so universal in the church today? The primary reason is to help families feel at home with preparing for and celebrating the sacrament.

It is also important for families to feel at home with the sacraments *in* their homes. The celebration of any sacrament is always meant to be communal. Receiving a sacrament is not just a personal experience between the child and God. It is a family event and a parish event.

This book has been written to help you to feel at home with the sacrament of confirmation by helping you understand its history, meaning, and ritual. It has also been written as a practical guide to help you extend the preparation and liturgical celebration of confirmation into your home through family activities and prayers.

Chapter One

Making Connections

"Do I have to come to the meeting tonight?" she spoke plaintively into the phone.

"Well, we're encouraging at least one parent or guardian to attend the information meeting if a student is going to be confirmed," I replied.

"But Kevin is my third kid. I've been through this twice before. I've already heard the pitch."

And I had already heard about Kevin! As parish DRE I had dealt with Kevin in my office several times and had heard the complaints of catechists attempting to teach him. "Kevin seems starved for attention," they would tell me. "He's the class clown—a bright kid who can handle the material we're covering, but he asks for a lot of attention."

Now Kevin had reached high school and it was time for him to decide about confirmation. "I don't want to be confirmed," he told his catechist, "but I have to be. My mom would kill me if I didn't get confirmed."

I knew all of this, and now here was Kevin's mother telling me she didn't need to attend a meeting for Kevin since she had done it already for his older brother and sister. I told her that some details of the program had changed since her last meeting four years ago. We were using a new book and had a special retreat program planned. The meeting was going to include some reflection about these children of our parish who were preparing for confirmation.

"I don't really care about any of that," Kevin's mother told me. "I just want him confirmed."

"Why?" I asked.

"What? Did you just ask me 'why'? I want him confirmed because it's time for him to be confirmed and I'm tired of fighting with him about going to religion classes. Once we get confirmation out of the way, I won't have that hassle anymore. Once he's confirmed he can stop going to religion classes and I can stop hearing about these meetings for parents!"

Kevin's mother had a point there. Certainly she was honest enough to say aloud what is unspoken in many parents' minds. In our country, confirmation often comes down to this—a sacramental requirement for teenagers, an event marking the end of formal religious education.

Of course, this is not what priests and religious educators tell us about confirmation, and it is not what I am going to tell you about it in this little book. But Kevin's mother was naming a reality. Even though confirmation is supposed to be about baptismal commitment, about dedication to the church, about reception of the Holy Spirit, it very often seems to be about ending formal religious education or even ending all ties with the Catholic church. Instead of looking like a sacrament of initiation, which it is, confirmation often looks like a sort of sacrament of *graduation*.

We Are Models for Our Children

If you are reading this book, you are concerned in some way with the preparation of a young person or a group of young people for the sacrament of confirmation. You are involved with a very challenging, yet very exciting and rewarding aspect of religious formation and faith development. Although, according to canon law, confirmation can be conferred at any age past the "age of reason," it is most common for parishes in North America to confirm students in junior high or high school. Therefore, you are probably thinking about the preparation of your son or daughter or a class of students who are adolescents.

How can we do this well? How can we convey the true meaning of the sacrament of confirmation to our young people? Can it really speak to their lives? How can we see to it that the celebration marks a new beginning rather than an ending of active life in the church? These questions concern all parents who are serious about the religious education of their children of junior high or high school age, and they should also concern all religious educators charged with instructing these young people in the Catholic faith.

The first question we must ask is whether we really believe that the Holy Spirit has any meaning in *our* lives as adults in the church. Do our baptismal promises, our own confirmations, the gifts of the Holy Spirit, or our call to holiness have any meaning for us today? Unless they do, there is little chance that they will have much meaning for our children. Children—even adolescent children—learn more from what they are *shown* than from what they are merely *told*.

When you brought your children to be baptized, you promised that you would raise them in the faith. For some parents this promise has led to a very active commitment. These parents have learned right along with their children. They were with them as they confessed their sins for the first time, and they see to it that their children receive the sacrament of reconciliation regularly. They brought their children to receive the eucharist for the first time and have joined them for Mass each week.

For other parents, "raising in the faith" has meant a more passive commitment. These parents have seen to it that their children received some formal religious instruction and have brought them to the church for the sacraments at the appropriate times. Their attitude seems to be, "Let the experts do it."

No matter how actively or passively you have promoted their faith development and religious education, you have lived with your children, enjoyed them, suffered with them, endured some difficult times with them, and loved them day in and day out. Now you have come to a different turn in the road, a time for decision making. The decision is up to them—will they make a commitment to the church? Will they recognize and celebrate the action of the Holy Spirit in their lives? Will they speak for themselves the promises that were spoken for them at baptism?

"What do you mean, 'The decision is up to them'?" exploded a father at a parent meeting. "I want my kid confirmed. It's my decision and I say she gets confirmed whether she likes it or not!"

Of course we want our children to choose confirmation. We haven't brought them this far to have them turn away and refuse this sacrament. However, we cannot force a sacrament on anyone—especially on someone who has reached the age of reason. A person who gets confirmed only because someone else says that he or she has to is probably not really confirmed at all.

In such a case the celebration of confirmation will almost surely mark the end of that student's ties with the church. It will be a ceremony endured, a commitment made with no intention of living up to it, a sterile experience done to satisfy someone else's sense of propriety. Is this what we want?

We want young people who choose to participate in confirmation preparation for themselves. We want them to celebrate a reality when they come to receive this sacrament—the reality that they see themselves as active, gifted members of the Catholic church who are responding to an invitation to confirm their baptismal commitment.

How do we accomplish this? Parents cannot do it alone, nor can religious educators or other members of a parish staff take all the responsibility. We who are adults in the church need to work together to show our children what the church can mean, how the Spirit acts in our lives, and why we have already made the commitment we are inviting them to make now. We need to work together to invite our children to join us in the adult life of the church, finding ways to make the invitation appealing and sincere.

We also need to be open to the possibility that some young people need more time to make a decision to be confirmed. It is not uncommon for some students to decide to wait a year or two. Parents worry that if their child waits, he or she will never come back for confirmation. It is gratifying to see how many who wait actually *do* come back.

"But my daughter didn't!" cried a woman I know. "She wanted to wait and eventually she walked away entirely. She doesn't go to church anymore. If she had been confirmed with her class she'd still be a Catholic!"

This woman sees confirmation as some sort of "net" that missed "catching" her daughter. She feels that there is a regular schedule for when things ought to happen ("with her class"). She also believes that a person who stops going to church has abandoned her faith once and for all.

All of us want our children to be happy. Many of us care a great deal about whether they remain practicing Catholics or not. But when we are realistic, we have to admit that we cannot live their lives for them. We cannot make their choices or walk their journey. We can only do what we have always tried to do—show them what we believe and how we live because of our beliefs.

This period of preparation can be a good opportunity for

us to spend a little time reviewing the history and meaning of the sacrament of confirmation. It can be a good time for us to reflect on our own church membership and our own spiritual life. This book is intended to offer some of that background and some ideas for your personal reflection.

Gifts

As I write this book, I am halfway through a year as a volunteer catechist at my own parish, preparing a group of freshmen in high school for confirmation early in their sophomore year. Recently our parish had a meeting for parents of high school students who have been invited to prepare for confirmation. Our pastor, our DRE, and we catechists all spoke about our plans for the confirmation program.

During my part of the presentation, I asked the parents to turn to someone other than their spouse and describe their child to that person. "Tell someone else about this child who is studying for confirmation. How is he or she a gift to your family? How is he or she a gift to our parish? What are your hopes and dreams for this child's life of faith?"

Many of the parents were baffled. Gifts? To our family? To this parish? Tentatively they turned to each other and began to talk.

"Of course there are negative things you want to say," I assured them. "Of course these children aren't always easy to live with right now. But tonight let's accentuate the positive."

I asked them to think back to this child's baptism day. What were their hopes and dreams then? How realistic were they? How have things turned out so far? (This was met with good-natured laughter.)

I hope you will do this, too. Confirmation sends us all back to look at baptism again. We ask our children, "Can you ratify what was stated for you when you were baptized? Can you say it for yourself?"

Is it enough to show them copies of their baptismal promises and ask them to repeat them before the bishop? What else was said at their baptisms? Have we told them of our hopes and dreams, of our prayers on that day that seems so long ago to them, but seems like only yesterday to us?

Part of our desire to see them confirmed was born on that baptism day. There is more to confirmation than a requirement. At its best, it is a renewal of a hope and prayer that this young person will continue in a life of faith. Typically, we adults need to renew our own faith when we begin to speak with our children about our hopes—and even our requirements—for them.

Over many years as a religious educator, I have seen young people get confirmed eagerly, hesitantly, mechanically, or even angrily. These different emotions directly correlate with how they have experienced membership in the church so far. How has church membership been lived out in their families? How have they experienced church membership as young people in their parishes? How have their gifts and talents been celebrated and called forth?

Why would anyone want to be confirmed in a faith that has made no perceivable difference in their parents' lives? Why would anyone want fuller membership in a church that has not been welcoming to them as young people?

My students and I are exploring the church together this year. We are meeting parishioners in a new way and offering our gifts to the church in ways that go beyond clean-up time after a parish dinner. We are "making connections" between promises made and lives lived. We are reviewing and learning the doctrines and rules and discovering how they, too, connect to our lives as committed Catholic Christians.

It is not enough for parents and teachers to send our children off on the exploration alone. We are invited to join them, to renew our own faith, to sharpen our own commitment. We are challenged to take a look at the connections between what we say to them and what we actually do.

Chapter Two

History and Tradition

From your own preparation for confirmation you probably remember studying and memorizing the seven gifts of the Holy Spirit. Perhaps you can still recite them today: "Wisdom, understanding, knowledge, counsel, fortitude, piety, and fear of the Lord." For many of us, this list of seven gifts is a precious tradition, a part of the body of information about confirmation and the Holy Spirit that we want to hand on to our children.

In fact, the list is taught in virtually every confirmation curriculum in use today, although in many cases a few of the more ambiguous words are translated more clearly, so that we have "counsel" called "right judgment," "piety" called "reverence," and "fear of the Lord" termed "wonder and awe in God's presence."

Rooted in Scripture

Where did this list come from? If you are old enough, you might answer that the list comes from the Baltimore Catechism. You would be correct, for these seven gifts are certainly listed in the valuable little reference book on Catholic doctrine that, for some of us, also served as our main religion textbook during elementary school. However, the list existed before the catechism. It is found, first, in Scripture, in the Book of the prophet Isaiah, chapter 11, verses 2 and 3: (A note in the New American Bible explains that the first mention of "fear of the Lord" was formerly translated "piety," describing how the catechism ended up with its traditional list of seven gifts.)

> The spirit of the Lord shall rest upon him: a spirit of wisdom and of understanding, a spirit of counsel and of strength, a spirit of knowledge and of fear of the Lord, [piety] and his delight shall be the fear of the Lord. (Isaiah 11:2-3)

Because Christianity has its roots in the Old Testament (now commonly called the Hebrew Scriptures), it should come as no surprise that every sacrament also has Hebrew roots and sources. Confirmation is no exception.

The passage from Isaiah cited above is a prophecy referring to the Messiah. In chapter eleven the prophet writes at length about how the Spirit "resting upon" this Anointed One will cause him to act. We are given a picture of a powerful leader who can make sound judgments and bring about a world of justice and peace. Chapter sixty-one of the same prophetic book begins,

> The spirit of the Lord God is upon me, because the Lord has anointed me. He has sent me to bring glad tidings to the lowly, to heal the broken hearted, to proclaim liberty to the captives and release to the prisoners....(Isaiah 61:1)

The authors of the Book of Isaiah expected readers of the time to recognize some key phrases and to understand their implications. There is no doubt, as we shall soon see, that Jesus was also a student of Scripture able to pick out such key phrases and use them in his own preaching. We who read the words in modern times are still able to recognize these phrases and make the proper connections.

One of the phrases is "the Lord has anointed me." Everyone hearing that phrase recognized that it pointed to priesthood and kingship. Isaiah's audience knew that the high priest, Aaron, and his descendants had been anointed with oil to mark them as spiritual leaders who were to offer sacrifice for the community in the Temple. They also knew that their first king, Saul, and all subsequent kings, especially their beloved King David, had been anointed with oil to mark them as political leaders who were to guide and safeguard the community.

They knew that oil was an important symbol of health and strength—a substance that provided them with light in their lamps, nutrition and flavor in their cooking, and healing and protection for skin subject to dry and harsh desert winds.

There are several sacraments of the church that include an anointing with oil, and confirmation is one of them. As they were in baptism, confirmation candidates are again anointed with the oil of chrism. It is placed on their foreheads in the sign of the cross, marking each one as a priest and a potential leader, a follower of Christ, the Eternal High Priest and King.

Another key phrase that gives a clue to knowledgeable readers is "the Spirit of the Lord is upon me." That picture of the Spirit of the Lord being *upon* someone is meant to conjure up images of resulting action. In both of the passages of Isaiah above, the Spirit who is upon the Messiah causes powerful and important things to happen—the poor are fed, captives are freed, justice and peace return to the land.

The people would recognize this from earlier passages of Scripture as well. In the First Book of Samuel, chapter sixteen, the story of the anointing of David describes Samuel's search among the sons of Jesse for the man God had chosen to be the anointed one. After looking over and rejecting seven splendid young men, Samuel asked Jesse, "Are these all the sons you have?"

Jesse replied, "There is still the youngest, who is tending sheep." This youngest son was David, and when he was brought into Samuel's presence, the Lord said "There— anoint him, for this is he!"

The Hebrew people delighted in this story of God's surprising choice and knew well what happened next:

> Then Samuel, with the horn of oil in hand, anointed him
> in the midst of his brothers; and from that day on, the
> spirit of the Lord rushed upon David. (1 Samuel 16:13)

The people were equally familiar with the results of the Spirit rushing upon David, their greatest king, who conquered enemies and secured their kingdom for them.

It was fitting that Jesus harked back to these same phrases and used these same clues to tell the people about himself. In fact, he quoted directly from chapter sixty-one of Isaiah.

The Gospel of Luke describes the event. Earlier in this gospel we read of the twelve-year-old Jesus confounding the learned teachers in the Temple. In the third chapter, Luke describes the Baptism of Jesus, and here, too, he uses the phrase "the Holy Spirit descended upon him."

Shortly after his baptism, Jesus returned to his hometown of Nazareth and went to the synagogue on the sabbath day. He stood up to read and we are told that he found the passage from Isaiah 61 mentioned above, which proclaims "The Spirit of the Lord is upon me." After reading the passage aloud to the assembled congregation, Luke tells us:

Rolling up the scroll, he handed it back to the attendant and sat down, and the eyes of all in the synagogue looked intently at him. He said to them, "Today this scripture passage is fulfilled in your hearing." (Luke 4:20-21)

It is wonderful to explore these passages from Scripture with confirmation candidates. They can identify with the young David who was chosen over his older brothers to be anointed for God. They can place themselves in the story of the boy Samuel who was called during his sleep and mistook God's call for that of his teacher Eli. Given the right presentation of these stories, they can hear themselves answering as Samuel answered, "Speak, Lord, for your servant is listening" (1 Samuel 3).

Our young people, like Jeremiah, can say:

The word of the Lord came to me thus: Before I formed you in the womb I knew you, before you were born I dedicated you, a prophet to the nations I appointed you.

"Ah, Lord God!" I said, "I know not how to speak; I am too young."

But the Lord answered me, "Say not, 'I am too young.' To whomever I send you, you shall go; whatever I command you, you shall speak. Have no fear before them, because I am with you to deliver you, says the Lord." (Jeremiah 1:4-7)

As they read this passage, our confirmation candidates can know that they are part of a long tradition of young people called forth from the community to be anointed, to serve God in some way, to feel that the Spirit of God is upon them.

There seems to be no doubt that these passages describing Jesus, kings, and prophets stepping forward to be ratified as leaders are passages that have influenced the practices that have developed into the sacrament of confirmation. Its scriptural roots are clear.

The Holy Spirit

Just who is this Holy Spirit who is spoken of so frequently, and who is received in confirmation? This third person of the Trinity, living in Divine communion with the Father and the Son, is often the most neglected aspect of our teaching about God.

Traditional church art has often depicted the Holy Spirit as a bird, a symbol taken from the story of Jesus' baptism when the Spirit descended upon him in the visible form of a dove. Scripture, however, also contains other powerful descriptions of the Holy Spirit—the breath of God, a mighty wind, a burning fire, a dancing woman. You may remember a time when the Holy Spirit was called the "Holy Ghost," a name that at times led to some interesting misconceptions.

When Jesus himself spoke of the Holy Spirit he spoke of a "paraclete." This word means "advocate," someone taking up a cause in defense of another. It also connotes someone who gives comfort to another. At the Last Supper, Jesus promised that he would not leave his followers alone, but would send the Holy Spirit as their paraclete. He further described the Spirit as a teacher who would instruct the apostles in all that they did not yet understand.

Perhaps the ultimate description of the Spirit "rushing upon" those who are called to follow Christ is in the Acts of the Apostles. Luke wrote this book as well, and he clearly ties the Spirit who is "upon" Jesus to the apostles' experience on Pentecost Sunday. The story is familiar to us:

> Suddenly there came from the sky a noise like a strong
> driving wind, and it filled the entire house in which they

were. Then there appeared to them tongues as of fire, which parted and came to rest on each one of them. And they were all filled with the holy Spirit and began to speak in different tongues, as the Spirit enabled them to proclaim. (Acts 2:2-4)

This descent of the Holy Spirit upon the apostles is often called the "birthday of the church." It is also considered another scriptural root of confirmation. (Clearly, it is not the only scriptural root, for the element of anointing is not included in this story.) There is no doubt that members of the early church saw this Pentecost event as a definite fulfillment of Jesus' promise to send his Spirit to be with his followers. The experience changed all who were present. Just as the Spirit resting or rushing upon someone in the Hebrew Scriptures was followed by extraordinary action, the early church could see that this descent of the Holy Spirit was followed by courageous and prophetic actions. The apostles came out of hiding and began to preach the good news that Jesus had risen from the dead. They began to form a community that served the poor and treated all with respect. They began to witness bravely and even to die because they were followers of Christ.

Those who wanted to follow Christ along with the apostles, those who wanted to join this community of believers, came forward and were baptized. At this point and down to this very day, there is confusion about just when the Holy Spirit is received. Did the Spirit come upon new Christians at baptism or later on within a further ceremony, the laying on of hands?

A Gradual Evolution
If you like history to be tidy with a definite beginning, middle and end, then the rest of this chapter—and any study

of the history of confirmation—could be frustrating for you. If you, like me, learned that a "sacrament is an outward sign, instituted by Christ to give grace" (Baltimore Catechism) and if you like to see exactly where and when Christ did the instituting, you are going to be disappointed.

The best that can be said is that the sacrament of confirmation has evolved over the centuries since apostolic times. There are passages in the Acts of the Apostles and in various epistles that indicate a belief that a person received the Holy Spirit at baptism. No separate ceremony or religious experience seemed necessary. At baptism a person was washed clean of sin, received the Holy Spirit, and became a member of the Christian community.

On the other hand, in several places this same book of Acts mentions a practice of "laying on of hands." The apostles, who had clearly received the Holy Spirit at Pentecost, found themselves able to confer that Spirit on others through this action. In the eighth chapter of Acts we read:

> Now when the apostles in Jerusalem heard that Samaria had accepted the word of God, they sent them Peter and John, who went down and prayed for them, that they might receive the holy Spirit, for it had not yet fallen upon any of them; they had only been baptized in the name of the Lord Jesus. Then they laid hands on them and they received the holy Spirit. (Acts 8:14-17)

In the early church, the action that caused the conferring of the Holy Spirit was actually less important to people than the results of that conferring. According to both scriptural and historical documents, the first century church was vigorous, lively, full of enthusiasm, and bursting with exciting activity. People were radically changed—often speaking in tongues, praying and singing together, living in communities and sharing all their goods, reaching out to the poor and needy, and being willing to die for their faith if necessary. Christians looked for evidence of the Spirit in one another and they found it. They did not really question when the Spirit had arrived. They simply celebrated the Spirit's presence among them, which they recognized by the way each member lived.

Baptism and Confirmation

The separation of baptism and confirmation, with which we are familiar in the modern church, was not always so clear. Today we refer to three "sacraments of initiation"— baptism, confirmation, and eucharist. Within the Rite of Christian Initiation of Adults (the RCIA), these three sacraments are conferred during one ceremony, usually at the Easter Vigil. In the Roman church, however, most people are baptized as infants, and confirmation and eucharist are separated and conferred at later dates. How did this evolution come about? How do practices differ from place to place even today?

Differences in practice existed between different local churches almost from the beginning. At first, two separate actions were always identified—baptism with water and the laying on of hands. Even then, the timing of the two actions differed from place to place. Sometimes they both occurred on the same occasion, but in some local churches baptism was conferred by local priests or deacons and at a later date the bishop imposed his hands on the new Christians to confirm the earlier baptism and to call the Holy Spirit down upon the new members. The practice of anointing with oil, so familiar to the Jewish community, was also added gradually from place to place.

When the church was young and small it was relatively easy for each local bishop to initiate all new members joining his community. Later growth of the church made it difficult if not impossible for bishops to continue to initiate everyone who joined the church. This was especially true after Constantine proclaimed Christianity to be the official religion of the Roman empire.

As the number of people joining the church grew, and as the church spread beyond the cities to the countryside, local priests and deacons began the initiation process by baptizing new Christians. Bishops traveled to local churches, or invited members to come to the bishops' churches at special times so that confirmation could be celebrated. The success of this practice varied from region to region. In some areas the common people had little concern for being "ratified" by a bishop. Though invited and encouraged to come for confirmation, they perceived baptism to be enough.

The gradual increase in infant baptisms, and the corresponding decrease in adult baptisms, also had an effect on the practice of separating confirmation from baptism. As early as the fifth century a fear of dying without baptism began to develop. During the Middle Ages, this fear grew very strong. Rather than connecting baptism with a period of learning and personal decision for young people and adults desiring membership, churches began to baptize infants so that they would be sure to enter heaven if they died before reaching a teachable age. Instruction in the faith began to follow baptism instead of preceding it.

In some locales infants were baptized and confirmed at the same time, but gradually the practice of delaying confirmation to a later age became more widespread. There were at least two reasons for this. First of all, church leaders still saw a need for the bishop to have a role in the initiation of every member of his flock. Confirmations celebrated annually made it possible for all who had been baptized to come forward at one time. And since infants were unable to speak the baptismal promises for themselves, church leaders saw a value in waiting to confer confirmation until those infants had reached an age when they could know what they were promising.

Just when that age is has been argued for centuries. Even today, the age for confirmation differs widely from place to place. Some of you who are reading this are concerned with confirmation of seventh or eighth graders. A few areas even confirm fifth graders. A growing number of dioceses, following the teaching of the church that baptism, confirmation, and eucharist are intimately related and are best celebrated in their proper order (with eucharist being the high point of initiation), have begun confirming children immediately before first communion. Others are confirming students in high school and some wait as late as senior year or even first year of college.

Exactly what happens at confirmation has also been argued for centuries. What is the theology of the sacrament of confirmation? We will explore this topic in the next chapter.

Chapter Three

Theological Reflections

For many years, theologians and religious educators have referred to confirmation as the "sacrament in search of a theology." Some authors have been disdainful about this, some simply resigned to the fact, and some rather apologetic.

What the phrase "in search of a theology" means is that the doctrinal, spiritual, and even liturgical definitions of confirmation have changed often over the centuries. Church teaching about this sacrament, as we saw in the last chapter, has changed radically. Not everyone in the church at a given time has even agreed on the theological meaning of confirmation.

Furthermore, the doctrinal teaching and the liturgical words and practices are sometimes not in agreement. For example, during the confirmation ritual the bishop prays that the candidates will receive the Holy Spirit. This at least implies that they have not received the Spirit before this time. But the church teaches us that we receive the Holy Spirit at baptism.

This confusion about confirmation can make people uncomfortable. Being "in search of a theology" seems a poor way for a respectable sacrament to be. It seems weak, vague, and maybe even embarrassing—especially when one wants to teach about it.

But why? Why shouldn't the church as a community of believers still be growing in knowledge and understanding of a sacrament? Is it so awful to be searching for a theology? It seems to me that it is a perfectly fine condition for a sacrament that for all times has been concerned with the action of the Holy Spirit, the Spirit who continually calls us to rebirth and renewal.

That part of confirmation's theology has not changed. Confirmation has always been about the Holy Spirit. Theologians may argue over exactly when the Holy Spirit is received—at baptism or at confirmation—but they all agree that confirmation is concerned with the action of the Holy Spirit in the life of the Christian being initiated.

Soldier of Christ?

The father of one of my students once remarked that "I learned that I became a 'soldier of Jesus Christ' when I was confirmed. I even got slapped on the cheek to remind me to be brave and to stand up for my faith. Don't you teach that anymore?"

Now there's an example of changing theology! That "soldier of Christ" teaching was very popular a generation or two ago, and in some places for a long time before that. In this case, it is also an example of mistaken theology. There is no scriptural or early church source for this teaching.

What seems to have happened is that as baptism and confirmation became separated, preachers needed to find ways to convince people to bring their baptized children back for confirmation. They began to stress the power of Satan and the need for a strengthening beyond baptism in order to overcome evil. A military metaphor was used by a preacher in the ninth century who admired the Emperor Charlemagne, and this imagery caught on. Liturgical practice also gradually changed because of this teaching about being a "soldier," and the original act of giving a sign of peace, which had often been a kiss on the cheek, was changed to a slap.

This teaching became so widespread that the catechisms and religion books had children memorizing, "Confirmation makes me a witness to the faith and a soldier of Jesus Christ." Many of you, like me, remember learning this. Perhaps you also remember the bishop's slap on your cheek more than any other part of your own confirmation celebration. That slap was the one action of that unreformed liturgy that had no sacramental character at all. It was a sign of peace gone violent, a liturgical action gone awry, and it was the most re-membered element for generations of people.

Baptism and Confirmation

The liturgical reform that began long before Vatican Council II and continues down to the present has sought to restore our sacraments to their original meaning and practice, and to renew people's understanding and appreciation of each sacrament. As we saw in the last chapter, such a restoration is difficult for confirmation because its early history is so unclear.

Those involved in liturgical reform, however, have pointed out that one thing about confirmation *is* clear: Confirmation is closely linked with baptism, and it derives its meaning from baptism. We cannot understand confirmation apart from baptism, even though they often are separated in actual celebration.

Liturgical reformers often argue for a restoration of the practice of keeping baptism, confirmation, and eucharist together as three sacraments of initiation conferred at one initiation ritual. In fact, this restoration has happened in the case of adults and in the case of unbaptized children who are entering the church after having reached the age of reason.

There are those who would like to see the three sacraments linked for infants, too. Others would like to delay baptism to a later age by enrolling infants as catechumens and then conferring the three sacraments of initiation on them in later childhood after a process of preparation and instruction. In fact, there are places in this country where these practices are now being tried. It is possible that someday one or both practices will be common everywhere.

In the meantime, however, most of us are confirming preadolescent or adolescent young people. Here, too, we must look at baptism for the meaning of this sacrament. We are no longer teaching children to be spiritual soldiers. The slap has been returned to a peaceful handshake between the bishop and the person being confirmed. Now we are asking our children to look back with us to what was said and done when they were baptized.

At baptism they received the Holy Spirit. They became members of the church. Their parents and the entire community promised to raise them in the faith, to instruct them, and to give them a good example to follow. The community stood and promised to reject Satan, to turn away from evil, to believe in God the Father, Son, and Spirit, and in the doctrines of the church. Those being baptized were washed in living water and anointed with the oil of chrism.

At confirmation the bishop imposes his hands on each candidate and once more calls down the Holy Spirit upon them. They renew their membership in the church. Standing before their parents and the entire community, they themselves promise to live the faith in which they have been raised and instructed. They promise to reject Satan, turn away from evil, and believe in God and in the church. They are not washed in water, but they are anointed with the oil of chrism.

Clearly, it is not correct to say that one receives the Holy Spirit for the first time in confirmation. From the moment of baptism the Holy Spirit is present. For all the years since baptism, that same Spirit has guided and inspired and been available for these young people. Confirmation does not begin a person's life in the Spirit. Instead, it acknowledges and celebrates it. The catechesis for confirmation and the celebration of the sacrament ought to call students' attention to the action of the Holy Spirit in their lives and invite a deeper response to that action.

The Presence of the Spirit

We adults who are involved in the preparation of young people for confirmation should also reflect on our experiences of and beliefs in the Holy Spirit. We say we received the Holy Spirit in baptism and confirmation. We sign ourselves in the name of the Father, Son, and Spirit. We decorate our churches for Pentecost and confirmation with bright red banners and bold white doves. With arms outstretched bishops pray over confirmation candidates everywhere:

All powerful God, Father of our Lord Jesus Christ, by water and the Holy Spirit you freed these candidates from sin. Send your Holy Spirit upon them to be their Helper and Guide. (Rite of Confirmation)

"It seems like that ought to make more difference," a woman remarked once in a class about this sacrament. "Don't you think it's sort of a shame that we don't get tongues of fire over our heads like the apostles did on Pentecost? How could anyone possibly know they received the Holy Spirit at confirmation? Do some people feel some powerful emotion? I don't remember feeling anything when I was confirmed."

This woman was correct to recognize that it "ought to

make more difference" that the Holy Spirit is present in this sacrament. However, she was looking in the wrong place when she tried to measure the Spirit by the level of emotion. During confirmation preparation, all of us—adults and our children—would do well to take some inner and outer "expeditions" to discover where the Spirit lives and how the Spirit acts.

Some of our explorations will uncover emotion. There *are* people who feel powerful emotions during prayer. There are those who pray in tongues or recognize some gift for healing or preaching within themselves.

Further explorations will uncover other gifts of the Spirit. St. Paul writes of the evidence of the Spirit in several of his letters. In 1 Corinthians 12: 4-6 we read:

> There are different kinds of spiritual gifts but the same Spirit; there are different forms of service but the same Lord; there are different workings but the same God who produces all of them in everyone.

The New Testament letters and the Acts of the Apostles are full of descriptions of these different kinds of gifts and service. We read of people called to preach, to care for widows and orphans, to provide hospitality, to heal, and even to die because of their faith in Christ.

As we saw in the last chapter, the early Christians looked for evidence of the Spirit's presence based on how individuals led their lives. Tongues of fire were not the proof they sought, but tongues praising God, hearts full of love, and hands giving service. It is clear that the Spirit's gifts are for *everyone*: Paul tells us that, "To each individual the manifestation of the Spirit is given for some benefit" (1 Corinthians 12:7), and that benefit is for the whole community.

What gifts do you recognize in the members of your

church communities today? Do your inner explorations uncover any personal gifts you have been given for the benefit
of your community? Do you bring a strong faith when you
come to worship? Do you share a generous heart with the
people around you? What gifts of personality, temperament,
interest, skill, or education do you make available for the service of God's people? When your children are exploring the
ways their local community is gifted with Spirit-filled people,
will they see you?

None of these are idle questions. They come to the heart of
what we believe or fail to believe about the Holy Spirit. At
each Sunday Mass we stand together and say that "We believe in the Holy Spirit." Most of us rarely give that belief a
second thought. Confirmation time in a parish is a good time
to reexamine that belief and to flesh it out for ourselves as we
teach it to our children.

The Spirit is given "to each individual," so we ought to be
able to recognize the Spirit in the people around us. Sometimes the Spirit seems obvious. A gifted preacher who in-
spires us all with a wonderful homily can easily remind us
that the Holy Spirit is alive and well. A soloist singing a med-
itation song so beautifully that we are moved to tears is
showing us the Holy Spirit, too. The Spirit is also acting in
every form of kindness and goodness that we see around us.
We can see the Spirit's life in crisp altar cloths laundered by
unknown volunteers, in bulletin announcements of meetings,
on the faces of people at prayer, and in simple words of
greeting.

How can we discover the gifts our own children are to the
church? How can we help them to discover their inner gifts?
When the Spirit of God "rushes upon them" will they know?

Recently I told my class how I have already seen the Holy
Spirit alive in each of them. They were amazed and proud
and a little shy. I have really seen the Holy Spirit by watching

these youngsters. Four of them are still altar servers even though the "tradition" of the parish is to stop serving after eighth grade. Two of those servers are paired up with young men who have mental retardation. They helped to train those men to serve and they continue to serve at Mass with them and to be their friends.

Three of my students are lectors. At a time in life when it is so easy to be embarrassed, they accepted the invitation to proclaim the Word of God to the community. Each time one of them steps up to the lectern, I see the Holy Spirit, though no tongue of fire is visible.

I see the Holy Spirit as one of my students plays her clarinet at liturgies and in her high school band. Another student serves as an aide in a religious education class. I even see the Holy Spirit in the difficult times—when a student who never participates answers a question, when a son and a father give a sign of peace though they disagree about a haircut or a curfew, when a daughter who wants to leave home stays and tries to make a new start with her family.

Service in the Community

Closely tied to the presence of the Holy Spirit is the concept of vocation, an important element of both baptism and confirmation. Vocation means a "call." In church use it means a spiritual call from God to serve within the community in some special way. It is unfortunate that in recent times the word vocation has acquired the more limited meaning of a call to priesthood or religious life. Within baptism and confirmation we recognize that everyone is called. Since all gifts are given by the Spirit to be put at the disposal of the community, every person has a vocation to serve the church in some way. All gifts are needed and all should be celebrated. This is stated very clearly in both the baptism and confirmation liturgies.

Confirmation of young people gives each local community an opportunity to examine how well they are calling forth the gifts of all members to be recognized, used, and celebrated in the parish.

In recent years, this element of vocation has led to the practice of "service projects" in many parishes. Those students I mentioned above who are serving and reading and aiding in a classroom are not doing those things as "service projects." They were invited by one or more adults in the parish to join in one of these ministries because someone recognized a gift in them.

There are no required "service project" hours in our parish and not all of our confirmation candidates are involved in any ministry or service at the parish or in their neighborhoods. We who are catechists work with these students to help them discover what they might want to do. We introduce them to people doing various ministries and invite them to see what the ministry is about and to join in if they want to. We also reflect with all the students on what their future vocations in life might be, praying with them to the Holy Spirit for guidance and discernment as they make future decisions. We teach them that confirmation will be one source of spiritual help for them as they make important decisions about their lives in the future.

Those parishes that do have required service projects can do this poorly or well depending on emphasis and explanation. At their best, service projects introduce confirmation candidates to the various ministries of the church. They are invited to join in the service activities of a parish organization in order to experience the rewards of sharing gifts with the community. Adults of the parish can serve as mentors and models. They can help the students experience such ministries as providing food for people in need, visiting shut-ins, helping people with handicaps, planning and participating in liturgies, teaching small children, and many other activities.

There is a theological question about the direction this common practice has taken, however. Inviting young people to participate with one or more church ministries is very appropriate, but requiring such participation as a prerequisite for confirmation moves us into shaky theological territory. A sacrament is not *earned*. A sacrament is a gift of the church, offered to its members freely.

Certainly, there are qualifications that need to be met for the reception of sacraments—age requirements, a required period of preparation, a proper disposition for receiving the sacrament, among others. Fulfilling a required number of service hours is not a canonical requirement for confirmation. In some cases it has become a local parish requirement. There have been occasions when young people have been denied confirmation because they did not comply with the service project requirement of their parish. In such cases, the focus has shifted from the correct goal of helping young people explore their own vocations as they are introduced to various church ministries, to the questionable goal of earning points or putting in time to prove their sincerity or worthiness.

Searching

As the sacrament of confirmation "searches for a theology," we are searching with it. The Rite of Christian Initiation of Adults that has been promulgated in recent years is teaching all of us a lot about both baptism and confirmation. This rite is not just for people who want to join the Catholic church. While certainly designed as a process for them to do just that, the rite is also for everyone in the church. Each part of the rite is celebrated in the presence of the parish community. The instruction elements also invite parish members to learn and grow in faith as they take on the roles of sponsors, spiritual companions, or instructors.

Every time we see someone take another step on the journey toward baptism we learn something about our own baptisms, about our own faith journeys. We remember that we have indeed received the Holy Spirit. We recall our own vocations and are challenged to strengthen and deepen our own faith. By participating in these ceremonies throughout each liturgical year, all of us in the church are learning more about what the sacraments really mean and how the sacraments can really make a difference.

Perhaps this "search for a theology" actually is a recognition that in matters regarding faith, morals, and spiritual life, we never stop learning. There is no "graduation." As this recognition spreads among us it will affect our children, too. When they see their parents and other adults continuing to learn, changing their minds sometimes, and deepening their faith all the time, young people will see a church that is attractive and vital. Confirmation could become what it is meant to be—a celebration on the journey, an important step in faith.

They will not learn this from what we tell them. They will learn from what they see us do and how they see us live. They will also learn from the ways we celebrate the sacraments—including how we prepare for and celebrate confirmation with them, as we shall see in the next chapter.

Chapter Four

Celebrating Confirmation

Several years ago I was working with a group of students with mental retardation. They were preparing for confirmation, and I was very conscious of their need for concrete experiences and for familiarity with everything surrounding the ceremony that they would soon celebrate. In our classes we saw, touched, and smelled the oil of chrism. We cut out pictures of our bishop from the diocesan newspaper and talked about his crozier and miter. We even passed around cotton balls so they would know that cotton used to wipe foreheads in church was not scary like cotton at the doctor's office sometimes is.

We did all this because those students had mental retardation. When I taught a class of high school students who were not retarded, I was busy with more important matters—such as exploring Scripture, learning about the Holy Spirit, and renewing personal commitment. These students, after all, were familiar with liturgical celebrations. I would go over the parts of the ceremony with them, of course, but I was not too concerned about giving them concrete experiences.

In a class conversation one day, however, I was taught an important lesson. As we read about the young David being anointed with oil by the prophet Samuel my students seemed dismayed to hear that Samuel had *poured* a good quantity of oil down over David's head. "Is the bishop going to do that to *us*?" a young man squeaked.

As I explained about the oil of chrism being placed in a small sign of the Cross on their foreheads, they all visibly relaxed. Suddenly I realized that the words "anointing with oil" that we had bandied about so casually were actually of very practical concern to these teenagers who care so much about their appearance. "Would you like me to bring some of this oil to class so you can see it up close before the ceremony?" I asked.

They were eager to see the oil. They began to talk about other concerns: Would the oil wash off easily? Would the bishop mess up their hair when he imposed his hands on them? Was it true that he wore a "weird hat," and why did he do that?

It occurred to me that while reconciliation and eucharist are part of regular parish practice, confirmation is an extraordinary ceremony for most people. In large parishes with many students to be confirmed, only close family members can get into church for the confirmation liturgy. Most of my students had never seen a confirmation liturgy or personally met a bishop. I realized that some of their hesitation about the sacrament was not from unwillingness to make a commitment, but from fear of being embarrassed. As long as we confirm adolescents these fears are going to be a factor. Of course, they are easily remedied by one or two informative lessons. It also helps to begin to celebrate the sacrament long before the day the bishop arrives for the actual ceremony.

Enrollment

Following the model of the Rite of Christian Initiation of

Adults, many parishes now have an enrollment ceremony several months to a year before confirmation. This is an excellent practice. At a parish Sunday Mass, students who are studying and preparing to be confirmed come forward after the homily to state to the pastor and parishioners their desire to be confirmed. The pastor asks the students what they want and they answer that they want to be confirmed. He then asks them if they will promise to prepare well for the sacrament, and after they so promise he invites them to sign their names in a book or on a document indicating officially that they are candidates for confirmation. Often parents, family members, and the whole parish are asked if they will promise to pray for the candidates and to support them by good example.

This little ceremony accomplishes several things. The importance of confirmation for the whole parish is emphasized. Students and parishioners alike see that the candidates are being set apart in a special way, pointed out as people on an important journey. Students also get some practice being in a "different" setting in church. Just as in the confirmation ritual itself, they are asked to stand up and answer some questions out loud, and they are being honored in a small way.

The enrollment ceremony has had a significant impact each time it has been celebrated in our parish. At one recent enrollment ceremony, we also passed baskets containing the names of confirmation candidates so that each person present could draw a name of a student for whom to pray in a special way during the year. We posted photos of the candidates on the parish bulletin board to remind people of these young people for whom they had promised to pray during the coming months. The general intercessions at Mass included a prayer for the confirmation candidates every Sunday. In many ways, our celebration of confirmation began long before the bishop arrived.

Some parishes include articles profiling each confirmation

candidate in their parish bulletins. Some print a regular update about the projects and activities of the confirmation candidates. There are many ways to emphasize the importance of confirmation for the whole parish. When one or more such activities are chosen, there is often a surge of vitality in a parish, a renewal of spirit.

What if you are in a parish where none of these things is being done? Perhaps you can suggest some of these things to someone on the parish staff. When a suggestion is made in a friendly manner it is usually well received—especially if the suggestion is accompanied by an offer to help with the project or even to organize it.

What do you who are parents know about your parish's confirmation program? Are there ways that you can get involved? Are adults other than parents also welcomed to be involved?

Sponsors

In the last chapter the question of "service projects" was raised. The service or vocation aspect of confirmation should also be part of the long-range celebration that precedes the bishop's arrival. How are the various ministries and organizations of the parish reaching out to young people, especially to confirmation candidates? What invitations are being extended to come and see and participate? In so many ways, the entire parish is "sponsoring" its confirmation candidates all during their time of preparation.

Of course, we have the practice of naming a formal confirmation sponsor for each candidate. Whenever possible, these people should also be involved in the long-range celebration. At the ceremony itself, the confirmation sponsor stands behind the candidate with a hand on the candidate's shoulder. Like the godparent at baptism, this person stands in support of the person being confirmed and as a witness that the candidate is ready to be confirmed. In most cases the confirmation sponsor is a baptized and confirmed Catholic adult. Often a baptismal godparent returns for this ceremony. This is recommended in some dioceses. In others this is discouraged because of the thinking that a new confirmation sponsor adds one more person to the system of spiritual support available for the candidate.

Some confirmation texts and programs promote the idea of having all confirmation sponsors be members of the candidates' own parish. The thinking is that the sponsors can then participate in classes, meetings, or retreats with the candidates. This works out well when it is done, but there are times when it means a lot to a family to have a particular relative or friend from outside the parish stand as the confirmation sponsor. Practices vary from parish to parish and diocese to diocese. Find out what the requirements for a sponsor are in your parish early in the time of preparation for your child's confirmation.

Who is your son or daughter going to choose as a sponsor? If you can guide your child in this at all, try to encourage the choice of someone who really is a good model, who would be a good spiritual support. Contact the sponsor about availability for the ceremony itself and for any other pre-confirmation events as soon as you know the dates. Of course it is possible to have a "proxy" sponsor, but what will that mean to this young person?

My class has started some required dialogue with their sponsors about faith and commitment. For some, arranging a conversation is as simple as walking across the street or stopping someone after Mass on Sunday. Others are writing letters to their sponsors or are calling them long distance. One student plans to use a tape recorder. For these students a sponsor can mean more than just a hand on the shoulder during a short ceremony. These people are being invited to truly be sponsors—to know the candidates a little better, to share their faith. By the time of the celebration, they, too, will have something to celebrate.

Retreats

Most parishes suggest or even require some type of retreat experience for each candidate before confirmation. Sometimes the retreat or day of recollection takes place right at the parish. When this is done, parents and sponsors can also easily be involved in part or all of the retreat. Sometimes students are taken away from the parish for a day-long or even an overnight retreat.

There are many excellent models for good retreats for teenagers. They often include dynamic speakers, contemporary music, small group activities, and other creative experiences. They are a far cry from the silent retreats we might remember from our early years. That is as it should be. There are good books to guide parishes who want to design effective youth retreats. In most areas there are gifted people available who can come in and provide such retreats for a parish or for a cluster of parishes.

Retreats are a good idea for all young people, but they are especially fitting as part of their preparation for confirmation. A retreat provides an extended time when students can focus on their personal spiritual lives, their hopes and dreams, their need for healing and strength and the guidance of the Holy Spirit. During a retreat the group of young people can become a community. Good retreat directors can guide them in activities that include and affirm everyone—even the shyest or most "outsider" students.

Parents and Peers

Becoming a community is an important issue. Young people look to their peers for support and approval, sometimes even to the neglect of their families. This is a natural tendency of adolescents as they begin to break childhood ties and move closer to adulthood. This need for peer support must be recognized and it can become part of effective confirmation preparation. The best confirmation programs do more than teach doctrine to the candidates. They provide a source of friendship and community for them.

This is an important point for parents. We are all concerned about the effects "peer pressure" can have on our children. What kinds of friends do they have? What stresses and temptations are in their lives? We want them to make good choices, to be safe, to be happy. A good confirmation preparation program includes opportunities to consider consequences of choices made and to be part of a community of other young people involved in the church. Once again, it is important for parents to know about the confirmation programs in their parishes, to understand what things are being offered to, or required of, their children, and to support the parish confirmation program.

Praying as a family is also important. But it is often very difficult to get teenagers interested in family prayer or faith sharing. It would be wonderful if you could schedule a nightly, weekly, or even monthly time for prayer with your confirmation candidate son or daughter. It would also be most unusual.

Even if your family already has a tradition of prayer times—at meals, before bed, in the car, on birthdays or other special occasions—it can still be difficult to maintain these traditions when children become adolescents. But if you do pray as a family, you have some built-in traditions that you can use during this time of confirmation. Simply including this son or daughter's name aloud during these prayer times can call down blessings and also let this child know how important you believe confirmation is.

If your family, like many families, does not have such a family prayer tradition, you should still think about celebrating this time before confirmation at home. Confirmation is an important parish event, but it is also an important family event. Teenagers are easily embarrassed when we say "too much," but they also notice and are usually quietly hurt when we say nothing at all.

A New Name?

One family conversation can center around the choice of a confirmation name. The custom of choosing a "new name" and being called by that name during the confirmation liturgy stems from the biblical tradition of a change of name indicating a new or renewed commitment to God. Abraham and Sarah, our parents in the faith, were called Abram and Sarai before they made a covenant with God. Peter was called Simon, and Paul was Saul before they became followers of Christ.

In the same way, for many years men and women who entered religious life took a new name as they began their new lives in the monastery or convent. The taking of a confirmation name is also part of that tradition. In some places it is still recommended or at least very popular to choose a new name for confirmation. Students are often asked to research the lives of some saints, to discover men or women with spiritual gifts that they would like to have, and to choose a confirmation name from among that group of saints. There are also students who choose a name or are urged to take a name because it is the name of someone dear to them—an admired relative or a close family friend. Sometimes a student will take the name of a sponsor.

In many locations today, however, the taking of a new name is discouraged. Students are urged to use their baptismal name at confirmation. It is easy to see why this has come about—as we have returned to an understanding of confirmation's intimate connection to baptism, the use of the name given at baptism seems most appropriate.

"But is it a saint's name?" is a question often asked. "Who is my patron saint?" ask the Kims, Heathers, Chads, Jasons, and other students with names that are not of obvious Christian or saintly origin. It is true that the name used at confirmation needs to be a saint's name. Sometimes the easiest solution is to find out what the student's middle name is. Both Heather Marie and Chad Joseph had immediate solutions to their patron saint problem. Sometimes a little research in a book of saints' names or in a Catholic encyclopedia reveals that there actually was a saint with the student's name or that the name is a derivative of a saint's name. Nancy, for example, is derived from Ann and so the patron saint for Nancy or Nan is Ann. With girls' names, there is also often a connection with the Blessed Virgin Mary. When this is the case, either the derivative name or the original saint's name can be used for confirmation.

Biblical names are also fine just as they are. Although Joshua, Deborah, and Judith are not called "saints," they were prominent figures in the Hebrew Scriptures and also prefigures of Jesus and Mary.

There are times however when neither first nor middle name has any religious connection. Tiffany Brie and Tab Butch are both going to need to choose a saint's name for confirmation.

It can be a lot of fun for a family to talk together and do a little research about names during this time of confirmation preparation. Reminisce with your child about why you chose his or her name in the first place. Find out what each family member's name means and who each patron saint is. Decide which of several Thomases, Margarets, or Johns will be your patron saint as you learn about each one's life and virtue.

Why bother about all this? Each time we recite the Creed we say, "I believe in the communion of saints." Catholic church teaching and tradition is strong about this—the saints who have gone before us are models in Christian living and can also be advocates for us in heaven. Such concepts can seem very alien to students of the late twentieth century, but when presented in a positive, enthusiastic manner students find the ideas intriguing and the research interesting.

The Bishop

Most of the time, when our sons and daughters stand up to profess their faith and to be called by those saints' names, they are standing before the bishop or an auxiliary bishop of your diocese. In some rare cases when the bishop is unable to be present, the pastor is given permission to confirm the candidates. The pastor also confirms adults and children who are received into the church through the Rite of Christian Initiation.

Students should be aware of who the bishop is before he arrives. In many places, students have written letters to the bishop telling him a little about themselves and saying why they want to be confirmed. In the best circumstances, the bishop will be able to meet the students personally either just before or just after the ceremony. As pastor of the diocese, all parishioners, including these young people, are a part of his flock. Most bishops welcome confirmation time as a good opportunity to meet people and to see each parish during an important celebration. In a few dioceses confirmations take place at the cathedral, the central church of the diocese. Here, too, the bishop will welcome the opportunity to meet all of the candidates before or after the liturgy.

The Rite

Confirmation may be celebrated either within or outside of

a Mass. When it is within a Mass, it takes place immediately after the homily, at the time when we usually recite the creed. The ceremony begins with the renewal of baptismal promises. These promises are made in the form of a dialogue with the bishop, who asks if the candidates will reject Satan, if they believe in God, in Jesus Christ who died and rose, in the Holy Spirit, in the holy catholic church, the communion of saints, the forgiveness of sins, the resurrection of the body, and life everlasting. To each set of questions the candidates answer together, "I do." At the end of these promises, the bishop proclaims these powerful words: "This is our faith. This is the faith of the church. We are proud to profess it in Christ Jesus our Lord."

The second part of the ceremony is the laying on of hands. As we have seen, this practice stems back to apostolic times. When the number of candidates to be confirmed is very large, the bishop extends his hands up over the whole congregation. When numbers are smaller, the candidates may come forward to have the bishop's hands laid on them individually. It is during this action that the bishop prays that the seven gifts of the Holy Spirit will be given to the candidates.

Now we come to the actual conferring of the sacrament of confirmation. This is done through the action of anointing on the forehead with chrism and through the words "Be sealed with the Gift of the Holy Spirit." Each candidate comes forward individually with his or her sponsor for this anointing, no matter how large the group.

Calling each candidate by name, the bishop says the words of confirmation while making the sign of the cross with chrism on each forehead. Each candidate answers "Amen" after his or her own anointing. The sign of peace follows immediately, as the bishop shakes the hand of the newly confirmed person and exchanges the greeting of peace.

A Family, Parish, and Church Event

Whether during or outside of a Mass, confirmation is an occasion for a solemn procession, for a beautifully decorated church, and for the best liturgical music possible. It is a "state occasion," marking with honor all of those who are confirmed, and pointing out the importance of this sacrament of initiation for the life of the church.

The life of the church, the spiritual life of our families, and the personal spiritual life of each young person being confirmed are all celebrated, blessed, and deepened when we prepare well for confirmation, and when we let its meaning become a reality for us.

While it is certainly up to our children to do their part in preparation, it should not be left entirely up to them. This is a family matter and a parish event, too. Students who get or are given the impression that confirmation is an isolated moment will go through the motions for us, but they will not be joining us wholeheartedly on the journey of faith.

Perhaps we have not been so wholehearted on that journey ourselves. It is never too late to begin. Baptismal promises *and* confirmation commitment can be renewed any time. Each time we teach or take time with a young person learning about the faith, we have an opportunity for such personal renewal. Each time we look at their lives and their commitment we learn much more about our own.

The students who step up to the bishop in our parishes on Confirmation Day will not be perfect. They are not members of perfect families or of a perfect church. But they can step up with confidence to be sealed with the Holy Spirit if they can tell that they are part of a community on a journey. When they can see us really trying to follow Jesus, when they can tell we are still learning and seeking answers, when they know that we make every effort to forgive one another and to live in peace, then they can say "Yes" to our invitation and "Yes" to their personal call from Jesus Christ.